EARLY AMERICAN TRADES
Coloring Book

Peter F. Copeland

Dover Publications, Inc.
New York

Special thanks are due Earl Hartman of the Edison Institute's Greenfield Village and Henry Ford Museum, Dearborn, Michigan, for originating the idea for this coloring book.

Early American Trades Coloring Book is a new work, first published by Dover Publications, Inc., in 1980.

International Standard Book Number: 0-486-23846-6

Manufactured in the United States of America
Dover Publications, Inc.
31 East 2nd Street, Mineola, N.Y. 11501

INTRODUCTORY NOTE

When immigrant craftsmen came to the American colonies, they brought with them a set of skills and a craft tradition that had its origins in medieval Europe. The New World offered the challenge of adapting old techniques to new materials and exigencies. It also offered unprecedented opportunities for the hardworking craftsman to become successful in a way that was denied his European predecessors. In the social upheaval of colonization, an inexperienced journeyman could set up shop as a master craftsman. Many master craftsmen (Benjamin Franklin and Paul Revere, to name just two) became members of a new aristocracy in the colonies, from which the statesmen and politicians of the young nation were drawn.

Numerically, craftsmen constituted 18% of the colonial population. This made them, next to the farmers, the largest occupational group. As in Europe, the master craftsman was head of a craft "household," which consisted of any number of journeymen and apprentices. The master craftsman supervised the work and training of members of his household. He also met and dealt with consumers of his products, taking their orders and anticipating their future needs.

To the colonial craftsman fell the responsibility of creating those innumerable utilitarian objects necessary for daily life. He approached this task with a competence and creativity that sometimes produced results of great artistry—witness the number of colonial craft items that have found their way into the collections of great museums. More importantly, the bewildering demands of the New World led to the creation of new craft forms that greatly facilitated the nation-building process. The Conestoga wagon, Kentucky long rifle and clipper ship were all innovations, essential to the developing commerce of the nation, for which craftsmen were responsible.

This book provides illustrations, rendered for coloring, of 22 crafts that were once commonplace in America, but are now rarely seen. Each right-hand page has a picture of an artisan (or artisans) at work at his craft. The facing page offers a selection of tools that he used and objects that he made. Several of the pictures are shown in color on the covers of the book. Each spread is accompanied by a caption which contains information about the nature of the craft, its colonial origins and significance, and other material of interest. Each caption also identifies the objects shown on the left-hand page, providing dates when these are available. It is hoped that, in addition to the enjoyment to be gained from coloring these pictures, this book will increase your awareness of the vital contribution these early craftsmen made to the development of this country.

PETER COPELAND

1. CARPENTERS, 1655. The indispensability of the carpenter is demonstrated by the fact that carpenters accompanied every expedition to the New World. Early colonial carpenters performed a broad range of functions, from the rough work of felling trees and hewing timber to the precise work of cabinet and furniture making. Urban carpentry became rapidly more specialized into trades such as rough carpentry, joinery, wood turning, carving, coffinmaking, coopering, cabinetmaking, looking-glass making, picture framing and wagonmaking. The carpenter on the left is finishing a panel with a block plane, while the man on the right is squaring a timber with a broad axe.

Above: **1.** nut auger **2.** brad awl **3.** broad axe **4.** hand screw clamp **5.** chamfer knife **6.** froe (for splitting a piece of timber into boards) **7.** framing hammer **8.** carpenter's plane (1770) **9.** bench saw.

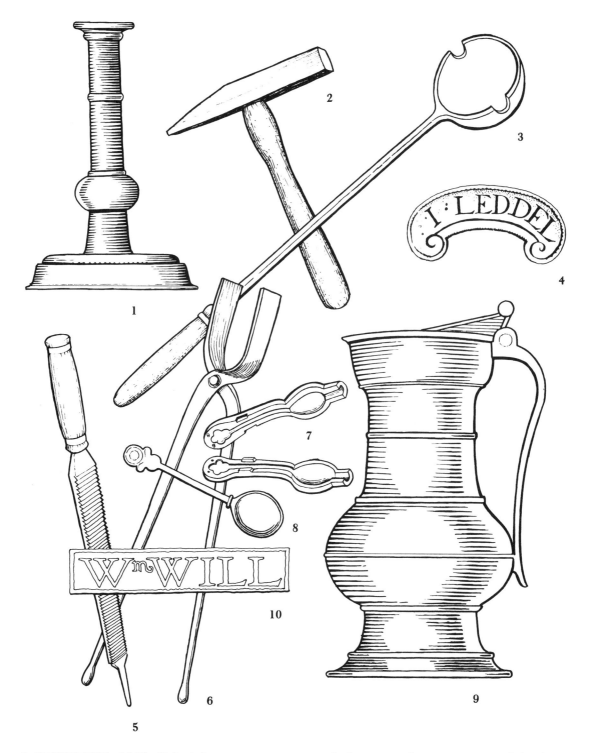

2. PEWTERER, 1695. Colonial pewter was composed of tin mixed 9 parts to 1 with lead or copper. The resulting product could be molded easily, and could be worked, when cold, without encountering the brittleness of other metals and alloys. Molten pewter was poured into a brass or iron mold, allowed to harden, and then smoothed with a float. A hand-powered lathe imparted a polish to the finished article. Pewter was used primarily to make utensils for domestic purposes, including bowls, plates, spoons, tankards, lamps and candlesticks. The pewterer seen here is pouring the molten alloy into a two-piece mold for making a dinner plate.

Above: **1.** pewter candlestick (1675) **2.** wedge-peen hammer **3.** molder's ladle **4.** pewterer's mark of Joseph Leddell, 18th-century New York craftsman **5.** float **6.** flat-bit tongs **7.** spoon mold **8.** spoon (1695) **9.** pewter wine flagon **10.** pewterer's mark of William Will, 18th-century Philadelphia craftsman.

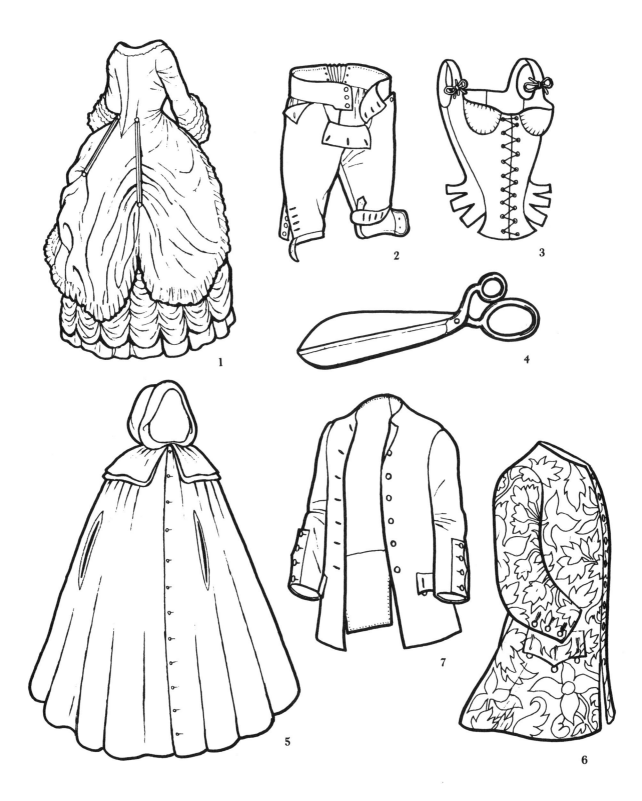

3. WEAVERS, 1733. In the 18th century, much of what was worn was manufactured at home, rather than purchased. Women and children would often perform the component functions of clothmaking: carding, spinning and weaving. Fine-quality fabrics and tailoring were reserved for the rich. Nevertheless, a thriving industry developed around clothmaking, especially among Irish immigrants, who were reknowned for their linen. This linen became a stock-in-trade of the itinerant peddler, who was a familiar figure on colonial thoroughfares. The woman in this picture is winding yarn onto a spool, while the weaver makes fabric on a foot-powered loom.

Above: **1.** lady's polonaise gown (1777) **2.** man's knee breeches (1775) **3.** lady's corset (1775) **4.** tailor's shears (1780) **5.** lady's mantle and hood (1745) **6.** gentleman's sleeved waistcoat (1730) **7.** working man's jacket (1775).

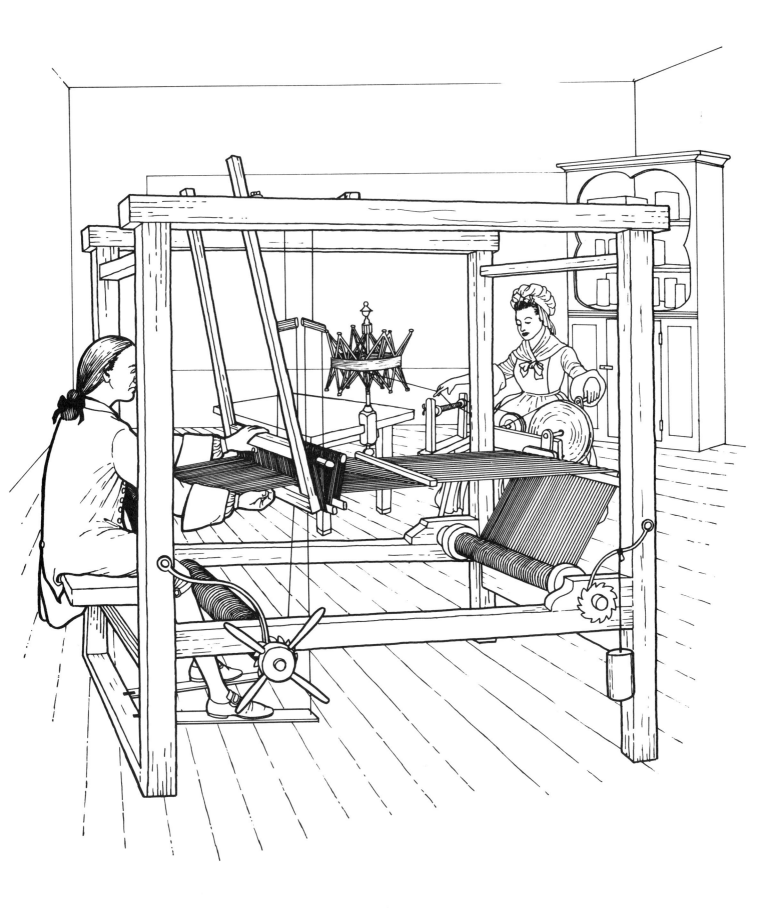

4. CABINETMAKERS, 1760. Cabinetmakers, or joiners as they were often called, were the most highly-skilled craftsmen in the carpentry trades. In 1700 an estimated 40% of the furniture bought in the colonies was made in England. By midcentury the amount of imported furniture had dwindled to an insignificant percentage. Indeed, cabinetmaking centers such as Philadelphia and Rhode Island were soon exporting large quantities of furniture. Many colonial joiners copied English styles (like that of Thomas Chippendale), but by the time of the Revolutionary War, distinctive American styles were emerging. The apprentice at the right of the picture is smoothing a tabletop with a block plane.

Above: 1. cabinetmaker's wooden clamp 2. forming chisel 3. open handsaw (1730) 4. miter box 5. T-square (1750) 6. sloyd knife (for scoring boards) 7. oak water bench (1850) 8. cabinetmaker's block plane 9. pine stool (1830).

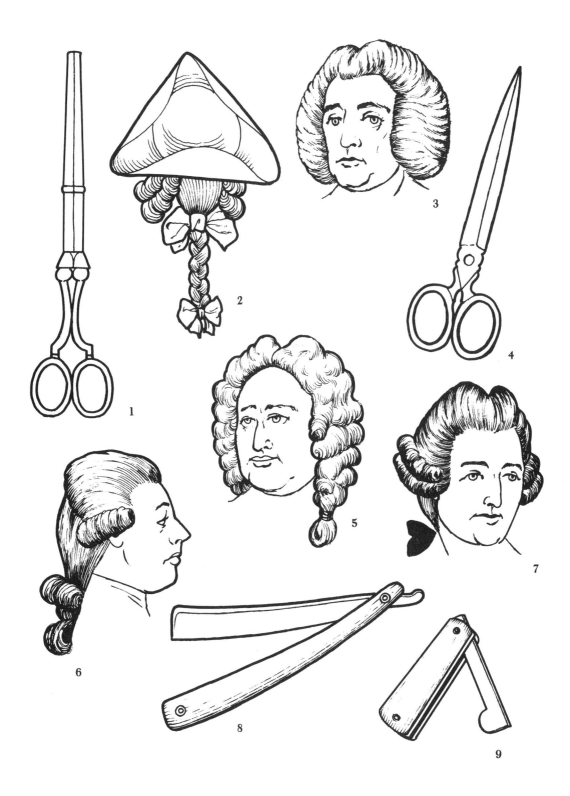

5. WIGMAKERS, 1760. Eighteenth-century wigmakers were also barbers, which meant that, in addition to making wigs, they often cut hair, shaved beards, let blood and pulled teeth. Men's wigs came in many styles. While the most expensive ones were made from human hair, cheaper ones were composed of horsehair, cow tails or various kinds of thread. Women began wearing wigs in the 1760s. By the end of the 18th century, wigs were rapidly declining in popularity. The woman in this picture is cleaning and combing wig hair, while the man is dressing the wig into a fashionable style.

Above: **1.** curling iron (1750) **2.** Ramillied wig (1745) **3.** physical wig (1755) **4.** barber's scissors (1770) **5.** campaign wig (1740) **6.** club wig (1770) **7.** tye wig (1772) **8.** razor (1775) **9.** barber's fleam (for letting blood).

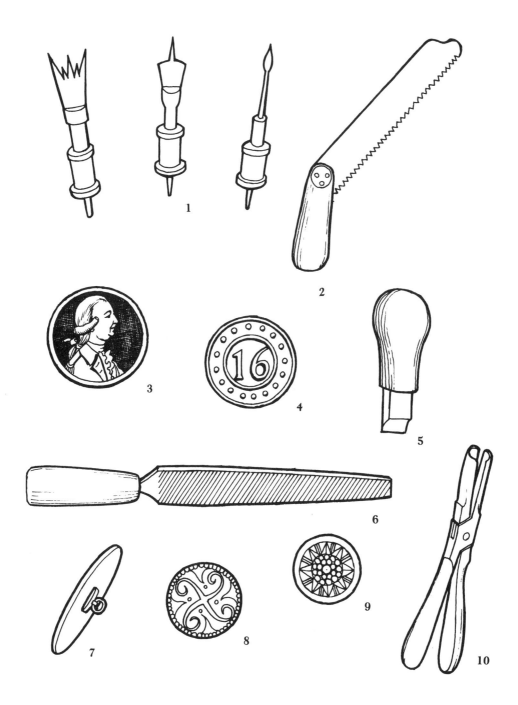

6. BUTTONMAKERS, 1765. Button manufacture in the colonies got a late start, due to the ready availability of imported buttons of all varieties. A factory which made brass buttons was established at Waterbury, Connecticut around 1750. The buttonmakers in this picture are engaged in making wooden molds to be used in casting metal buttons. The man and woman in the foreground are producing rough molds using a drill bit which is turned by means of a bow. The workers in the background are finishing the molds using a drill which attains very high speeds due to the difference in the size of the wheels. Various drill bits can be seen in the rack on the wall.

Above: **1.** three drill bits **2.** buttonmaker's saw **3.** portrait button (1775) **4.** pewter military button (1777) **5.** chisel **6.** file **7.** back of a silver button **8.** brass coat button (1750) **9.** gold shirt button (1780) **10.** pliers.

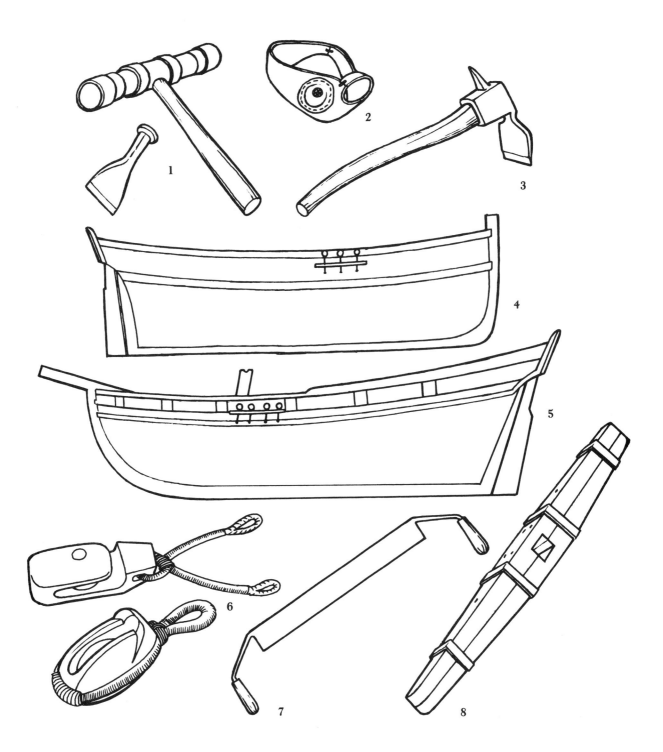

7. SHIPWRIGHTS, 1765. Shipbuilding was an exceedingly complex craft, employing the services of as many as 30 different kinds of craftsmen, representing the entire spectrum of colonial trades. So successful were colonial shipwrights, that by 1774, one-third of all vessels flying the English flag had been made in colonial shipyards, mainly in Boston, Portsmouth, Salem, Newport and Philadelphia. It took a year of hard labor, mainly specialized carpentry, to frame and finish a bulky ship. The scarcity of hardware meant that fittings and even nails had to be made of wood. The shipwright on the left of this picture is driving treenails (wooden pegs) to secure the outer planking of a small schooner.

Above: **1.** ironbound wooden mallet and caulking iron **2.** sailmaker's palm (for sewing sail canvas) **3.** ship carpenter's adze **4.** fishing smack **5.** Bermuda sloop **6.** ship's blocks **7.** mast drawknife **8.** ironbound wooden anchor stock.

8. SILVERSMITHS, 1767. Because there were few safe places to keep money, wealthy colonists often had their silver coin converted into household silver such as tankards, bowls, teapots and silver tableware. Silver objects could be marked with an owner's name or initials for greater security. The silversmith on the right is pouring molten silver into a crucible, or mold. The smiths on the left are beating out a plate of silver on an anvil.

Above: **1.** crucible **2.** spoon die **3.** flatting hammer **4.** calipers (for applying silver leaf) **5.** scissors in a silver case (1790) **6.** brazier **7.** touchmark (maker's mark) of Thauvet Besley, 18th-century New York silversmith **8.** silver basting spoon (1750) **9.** silver bowl (1736).

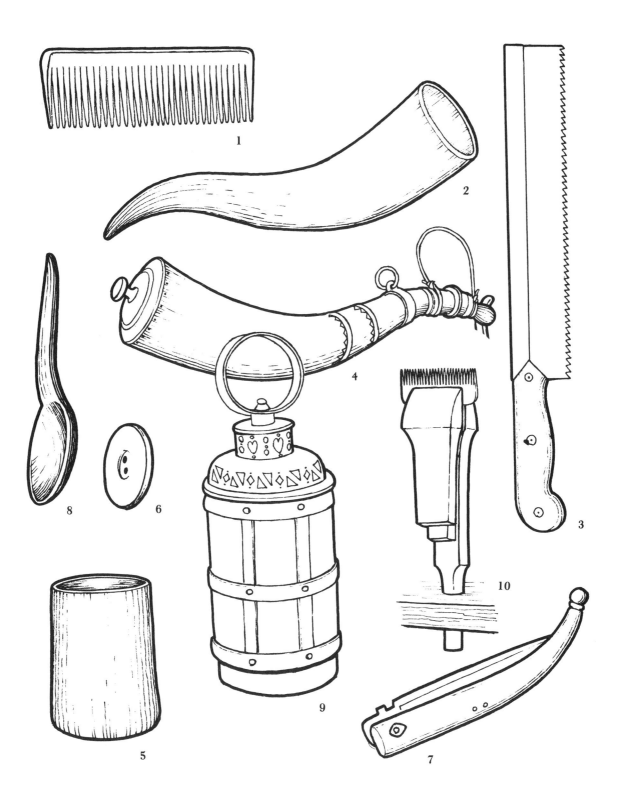

9. HORNSMITHS, 1770. In colonial times horn was a common material with which to make buttons, combs, handles, cups and spoons. The industry was centered at Leominster, Massachusetts, where it began to flourish around 1760. Hornsmiths also worked in tortoise shell imported from the Bahamas, to produce a class of goods more expensive than those made from cow horn. Horn had to be split, boiled and pressed before it could be worked. The picture shows a pair of hornsmiths engaged in making combs, which were the most popular item made from horn. Horn is pressed in the machine seen in the background.

Above: **1.** horn comb **2.** cow horn before being worked **3.** saw **4.** powder horn **5.** horn cup **6.** horn button **7.** jacknife with horn handles (1760) **8.** horn spoon **9.** lantern with horn lenses **10.** comb vise.

10. PRINTERS, 1775. The first book printed in the colonies was published at Harvard College in 1640; the first newspaper, in Boston in 1690. Like Benjamin Franklin, the colonial printer not only printed a newspaper, but also acted as its publisher and editor. In addition to printing books and newspapers, the printer supplied his community with business papers, legal forms and handbills, and frequently acted as postmaster. The apprentice seen on the right is inking type on a stone slab preparatory to a press run. The master printer on the left is inspecting a proof sheet.

Above: 1. composing stick 2. punch 3. counterpunch 4. imposing stone 5. cast type 6. type specimen (1723) 7. leather-bound book with brass catches (1660) 8. compositor's desk.

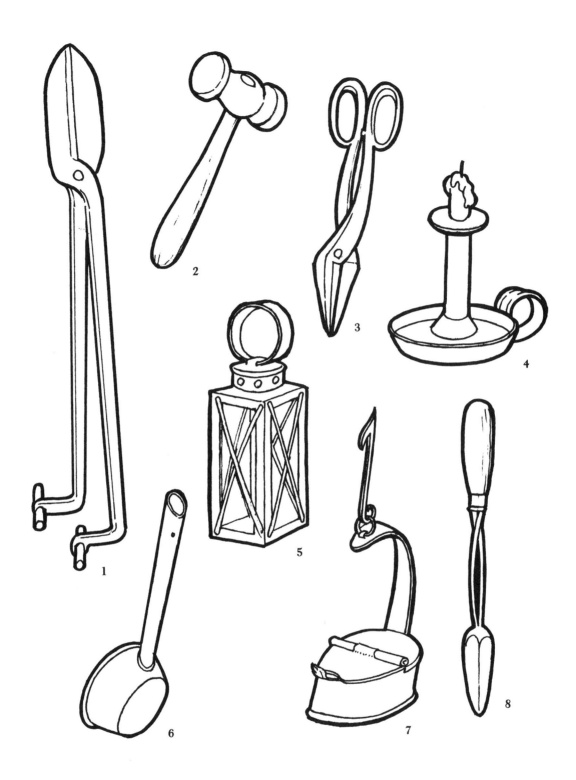

11. WHITESMITH, 1776. Colonial tinsmithing, called whitesmithing, got its start in the 1730s in Berlin, Connecticut, when Irish immigrants began importing sheet tin from England. This material was really thin sheet iron, plated with tin to prevent rust. By beating out their own kitchen utensils using wooden mallets, these whitesmiths could manufacture a product that easily undersold the spoons, cups, pots and pans that were imported from England. Berlin remained the center of the tin industry until the mid-19th century. Whitesmithing gave rise to another group of tradesmen who became a common sight in early America: itinerant tin peddlers. The smith in this picture is smoothing a cylinder with a wooden mallet on an iron former.

Above: **1.** anchored shears **2.** flatting hammer **3.** tin snips **4.** tin candlestick (1760) **5.** tin lantern (1775) **6.** tin dipper **7.** tin Betty lamp (1790) **8.** soldering iron.

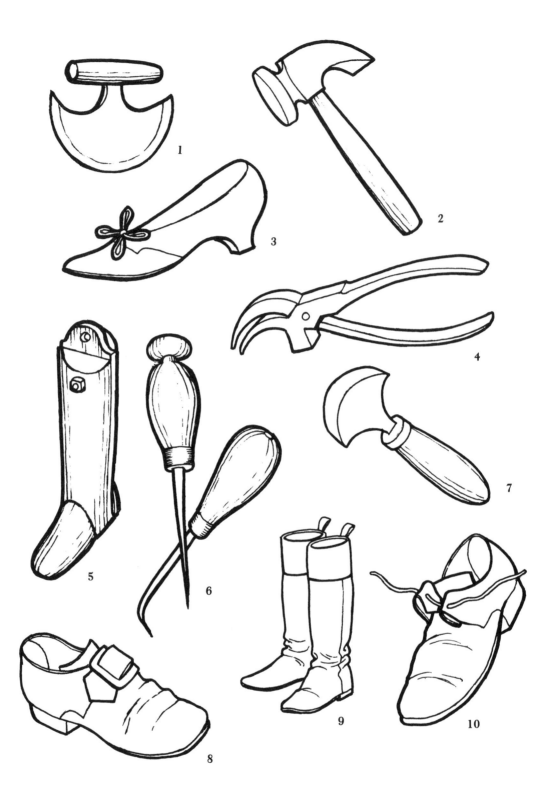

12. SHOEMAKER, 1780. The first shoemaker, or cordwainer, in the American colonies was probably Thomas Beard, who arrived at Plymouth, Massachusetts aboard the *Mayflower* in 1629. Although the wealthiest colonists often imported their boots from England, shoemaking was still a thriving trade. The cordwainer's shop was usually a small one, with little in the way of machinery. Seen here is a craftsman at his bench, with wooden lasts, used for forming shoes, arranged on the wall behind him.

Above: **1.** sole knife **2.** shoemaker's hammer **3.** lady's shoe (1800) **4.** stretcher pliers **5.** boot last **6.** awls **7.** burnisher **8.** man's buckled shoe (1776) **9.** riding boots (1776) **10.** man's laced shoe (1780).

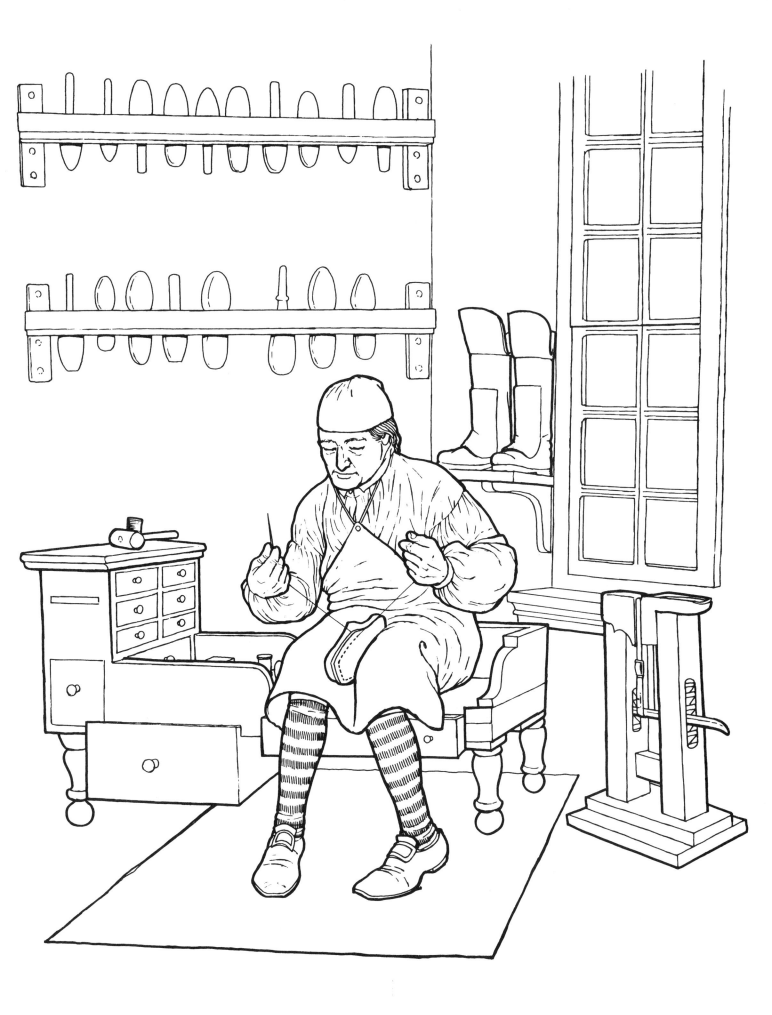

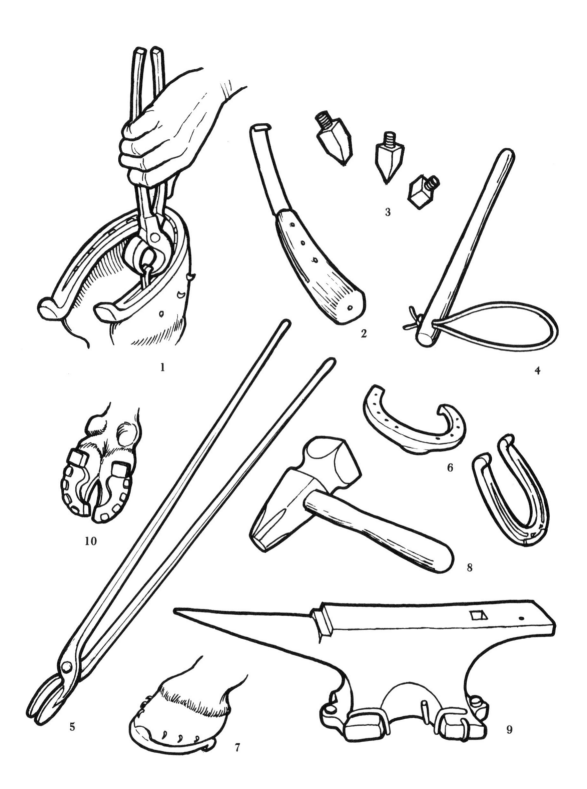

13. FARRIERS; 1785. The farrier shoed horses and oxen with iron shoes made at his own forge. He also performed many of the functions of the modern veterinarian. He would inspect an animal's feet and legs, looking for an injury or cracked hooves. The farrier used a "twitch" to discipline a refractory animal and make it submit to shoeing. The two farriers in this picture are doing a job often performed by one man alone. The forge and bellows can be seen in the background. The farrier's functions overlapped with those of the blacksmith.

Above: **1.** pulling an old horseshoe **2.** farrier's drawing knife **3.** screw calks (fastened to winter shoes for working on ice) **4.** twitch **5.** horseshoe tongs **6.** horseshoes **7.** horse's hoof with finished shoe **8.** farrier's set hammer **9.** anvil **10.** ox shoe.

14. GLASSBLOWERS, 1785. The first glass of American manufacture was made at Jamestown, Virginia in 1609, but the industry did not begin to thrive until 1737, when a factory was established near Salem, New Jersey for the production of window glass, lamp glass, snuff canisters and bottles. Later, Leyden jars (early devices for storing electricity) were made at the suggestion of Benjamin Franklin. The man on the left in the picture is shaping the lip on a bottle. On the right is an iron-topped table called a "marver," on which hot glass is rolled into shape prior to blowing a bottle.

Above: **1.** stirrer **2.** skimmer **3.** wooden tweezers **4.** neck-forming shears **5.** glassmaker's hammer **6.** wine glass with pedestal stem (1770) **7.** bottle (1730) **8.** bottle (1770) **9.** sweetmeat glass (1770) **10.** glass furnace shovel.

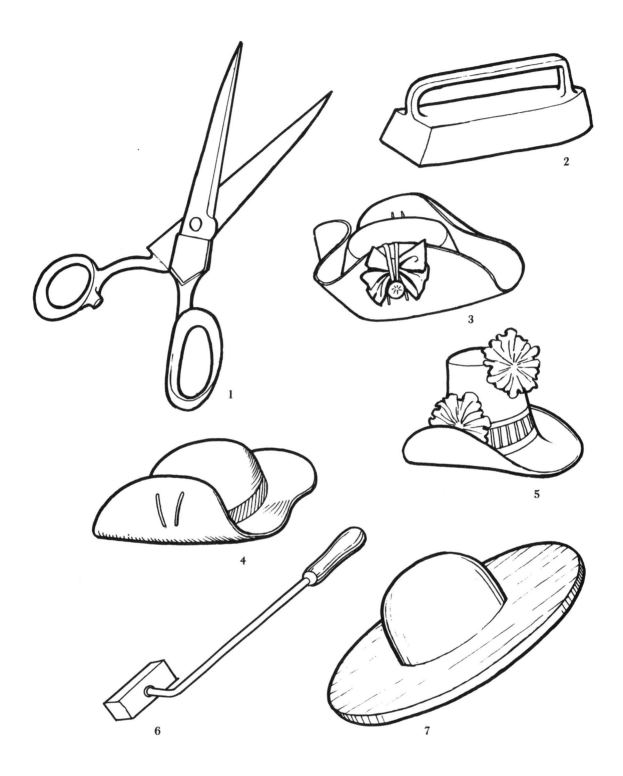

15. HATTERS, 1787. Though an English law, known as the Hat Act, tried to restrict hatmaking in the colonies, it was generally ignored. The best hats of the 18th and 19th centuries were made from beaver fur. The fur was shaved from the pelts, matted together and boiled in acid. It was then beaten and planked (cut to size) to create felt. The hatter on the right is preparing a wooden block, which is used to shape the hats. The man on the left is stacking hats that have been blocked, and are ready for the final shaping.

Above: **1.** hatter's shears **2.** hatter's iron **3.** soldier's cocked hat (1779) **4.** workingman's round hat, cocked in front (1775) **5.** lady's riding hat (1790) **6.** tacking iron **7.** wooden hat block (1760).

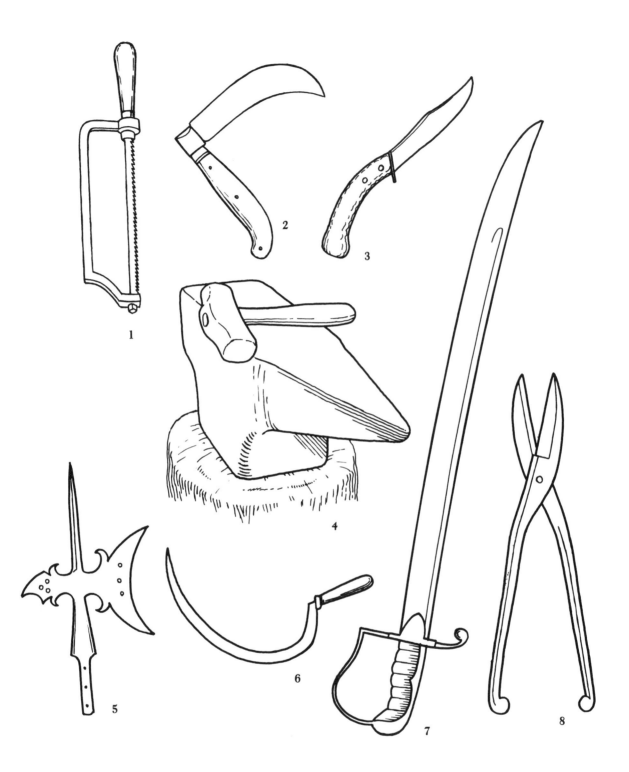

16. CUTLERS, 1788. The cutler was a specialized type of blacksmith who used steel to fashion implements, weapons and tools with a cutting edge. This trade really got underway about 1730, when the first steel furnaces were opened in the colonies. However, imported cutlery remained very competitive with the domestically produced variety as late as the 1830s. The craftsman at left of the picture is turning a grinding wheel for the cutler at the right, who is sharpening a knife. The forge and bellows may be seen in the background.

Above: **1.** hacksaw **2.** claspknife (1770) **3.** rifleman's knife (1790) **4.** cutler's anvil and maul hammer **5.** halberd (1776) **6.** sickle **7.** horseman's saber (1812) **8.** cutler's snips.

17. COOPER, 1818. Farmers, especially those in the South, needed millions of barrels per year to store and export crops and commodities such as flour, corn meal and molasses. This made coopering one of the most prevalent trades in pre- and post-revolutionary America. Mainly using oak, coopers made and mended barrels, kegs, buckets, tubs and tankards. There were "dry" barrels for dry goods and "wet" barrels for liquid items. The cooper seen here is assembling the staves of a barrel, preliminary to fastening the barrel together with hickory hoops. A cooper could make ten barrels per day by this method.

Above: **1.** sun plane (with a curved surface) **2.** pod auger **3.** wooden tankard **4.** croze (for cutting grooves) **5.** compass **6.** hand adze **7.** barrel (1740) **8.** keeler (1830).

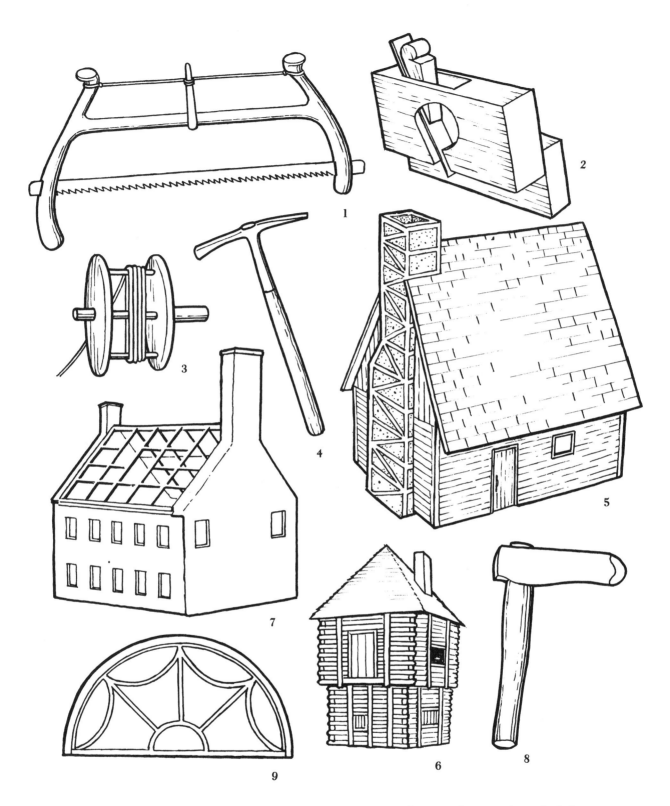

18. HOUSEWRIGHTS, 1819. Housewrights were master craftsmen whose trade included architecture as well. Early colonial house and public architecture resembled that of northern Europe, until about 1700, when indigenous styles began to emerge. Oak, which was in plentiful supply, was the primary construction material. Houses were fastened together with wooden pegs, called treenails. The man on the left of the picture is squaring a log with a broad axe, while the man on the right is smoothing a beam with an adze.

Above: **1.** handsaw **2.** rabbit plane **3.** chalk line reel **4.** trimmer's hammer **5.** Plymouth, Massachusetts house (1627) **6.** blockhouse (1770) **7.** Quebec house (1759) **8.** mortise axe (for cutting square holes for joints) **9.** fan sash for a doorway (1804).

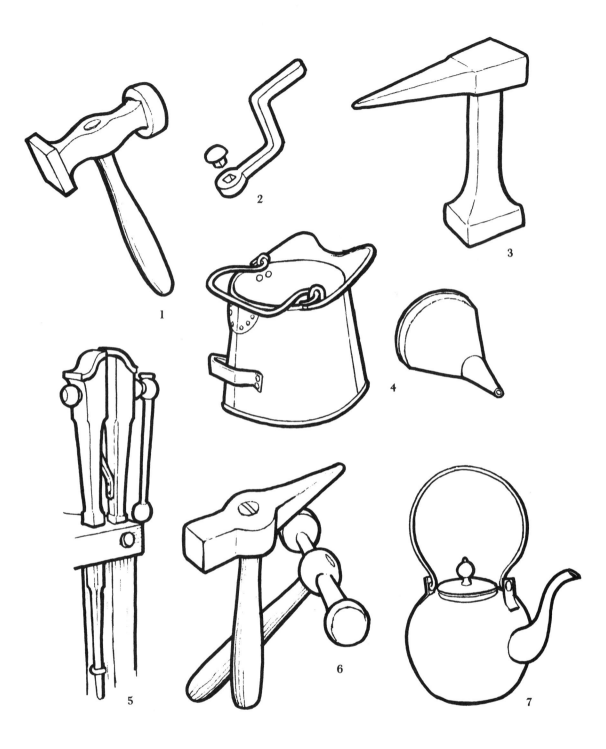

19. COPPERSMITH, 1838. In the early 18th century copper mines were operating in Connecticut, Pennsylvania and New Jersey, yielding ores of good quality. Although it was an important export product, much of the copper was used by American craftsmen to manufacture cups, pots, utensils and various fittings of copper and brass. Among the coppersmith's most important products were the large copper kettles used by other craftsmen, such as hornsmiths, hatters and dyers. Shown here is a coppersmith at work at his bench, with a forge and hand-operated bellows in the background.

Above: **1.** planishing hammer **2.** cranked horse (a type of clamp) **3.** iron bickern (for forming small copper objects) **4.** copper whiskey measure and funnel **5.** coppersmith's vice **6.** bumping hammers **7.** copper kettle (1850).

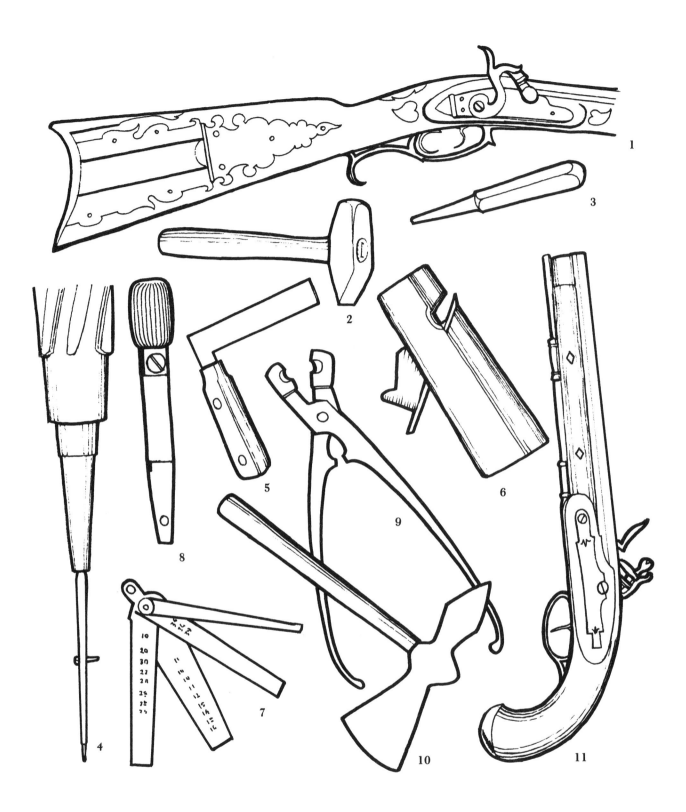

20. GUNSMITH, 1840. As pioneers moved west in the years following the American Revolution, the demand for guns increased. The most well-known arm manufactured during this period was the Kentucky rifle, many of which were built in and around Lancaster County, Pennsylvania. These rifles were fired by means of a percussion lock, which replaced the earlier flintlock devices. The gunsmith made his own gun barrels by wrapping hot iron bands around a cylindrical rod, and then driving the rod back out of the formed barrel. In the late 19th century, mass production methods replaced traditional gunsmithing.

Above: **1.** butt, patchbox and percussion lock of a long rifle (1830) **2.** riveting hammer **3.** punch **4.** scribe **5.** try square **6.** plane **7.** barrel gauge **8.** cherry (for making bullet molds) **9.** bullet mold (1840) **10.** trade axe **11.** Kentucky flintlock pistol (1812).

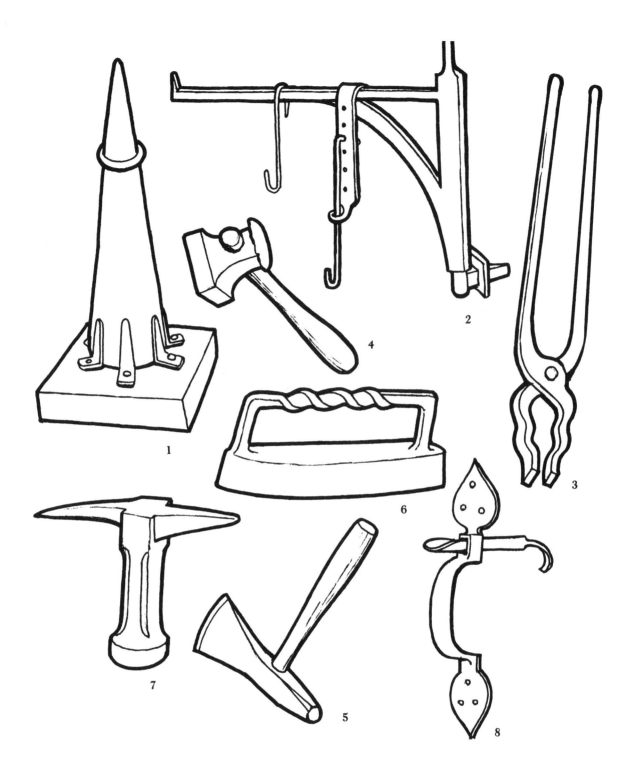

21. BLACKSMITH, 1840. Beginning in 1715, pig and bar iron were manufactured in Massachusetts and Connecticut. The establishment of this key industry, a great source of Yankee pride, was an important factor in enabling the colonies to become independent of England. These furnaces furnished raw materials for the blacksmith, who, in turn, provided iron tools for use by craftsmen and farmers. Indeed, the early blacksmith made everything that could be made of iron by hand: weapons, cooking utensils, horseshoes, cutlery, even padlocks. Eventually, many of these functions were taken over by more-specialized craftsmen such as locksmiths, cutlers and farriers; but even today, the all-purpose blacksmith can be seen in some rural communities.

Above: **1.** cone mandrel (for making iron rings) **2.** fireplace crane **3.** pick-up tongs **4.** flatter **5.** hot set **6.** flatiron (1840) **7.** bickern (for shaping hot iron) **8.** door latch.

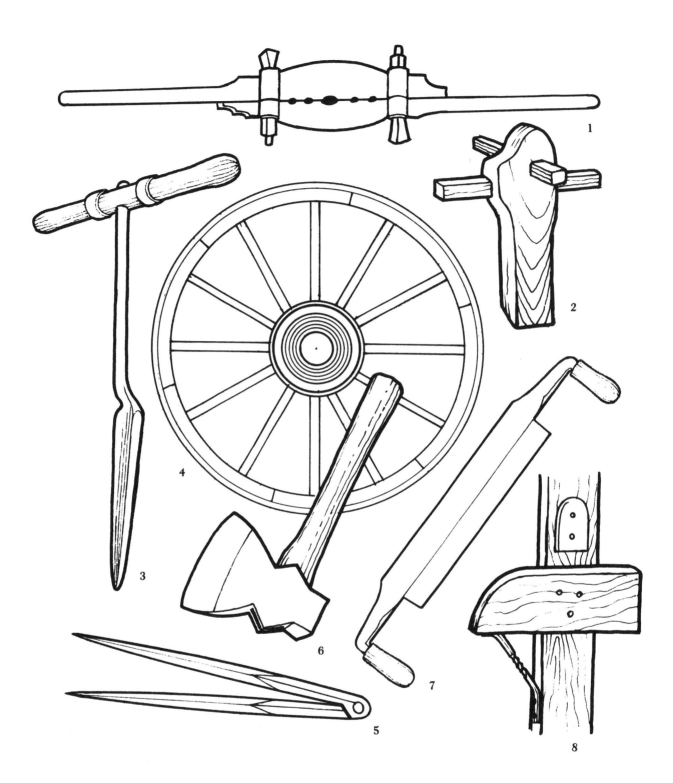

22. WHEELWRIGHT AND WAINWRIGHT, 1855. The wheelwright made and repaired wheels for wagons, carts, carriages and coaches. His counterpart in this enterprise was the wainwright (seen in the background), who made the rest of the vehicle. Perhaps their most notorious product was the Conestoga covered wagon, or prairie schooner, which greatly facilitated the westward expansion of the United States. This wagon, invented in the Conestoga Valley of Pennsylvania by German immigrants, had a long, deep bed, with a sag in the middle that made the load shift toward the middle on inclines. The wheelwright in this picture is fitting the felloes on the spokes of a wheel, using a spoke dog to strain two spokes together.

Above: **1.** screw die (for cutting threads on a wooden dowel) **2.** wheelwright's gauge **3.** wheelwright's hooked reamer (for enlarging holes) **4.** Conestoga wagon wheel **5.** compass **6.** broad hatchet **7.** wagonmaker's draw knife **8.** post tire bender.